STAR WARS®
REVENGE OF THE SITH
SCRAPBOOK

Written by Ryder Windham

SCHOLASTIC

Contents

Introduction	3
The Jedi	4
Jedi Equipment	6
Mace Windu and Yoda	8
The Jedi Council	10
The Sith	12
Clone Wars Villains	14
Separatist Droid Armies	16
Trade Federation Droid Army	18
Republic Clone Trooper Army	20
Clone Commanders	22
The Senate	24
Senator Padmé Amidala	26
The Delegation of Two Thousand	28
C-3PO and R2-D2	30
Utapau	32
Kashyyyk	34
Wookiee Origins	36
Polis Massa	38
Mustafar	40
The Epic Battle	42
Darth Vader	44
Jedi in Hiding	46

Scholastic Children's Books, Commonwealth House, 1-19 New Oxford Street, London WC1A 1NU. A division of Scholastic Ltd.

First published in the USA by Random House Children's Books, a division of Random House, Inc., New York, 2005

This edition first published in the UK by Scholastic Ltd, 2005

1 2 3 4 5 6 7 8 9 10. Printed by Proost, Belgium

www.starwars.com

INTRODUCTION

In the 1977 release of *Star Wars,* Darth Vader's frightful black-armored form stepped into the white corridor of the captured Rebel starship. It appeared that director George Lucas's story consisted of simple contrasts: light and dark, heroes and villains, good and evil. But the contrasts took on an added dimension later in the film, when the noble Jedi Knight Obi-Wan Kenobi disclosed that Vader had been his apprentice before turning to the dark side.

The Empire Strikes Back (1980) and *Return of the Jedi* (1983) revealed more information about Darth Vader's past, including that his name had once been Anakin Skywalker. But how did this former Jedi become a murderous, bionic Sith Lord?

To answer that question, Lucas returned to the saga's beginning. *Star Wars*: Episode I *The Phantom Menace* (1999) explained how Anakin— then a bright nine-year-old boy—became Obi-Wan's apprentice. *Star Wars*: Episode II *Attack of the Clones* (2002) showed twenty-year-old Anakin's difficulty with Jedi ways, especially controlling his sometimes volatile emotions.

During the making of *Attack of the Clones,* Lucas acknowledged that Episode III would "probably be the darkest of all of them." This was inevitable. The very first film (retitled *Star Wars*: Episode IV *A New Hope*) had already established the chain of events: the Republic will fall, the Empire will rise, and Darth Vader will emerge.
Brace yourself for . . .

REVENGE OF THE SITH™

The Jedi

The ancient Jedi originated as a philosophical study group who contemplated the mysterious energy field called the Force. Using the Force to help those in need, the Jedi have been the peacekeepers of the Galactic Republic for 25,000 years. Now that the Confederacy of Independent Systems threatens the freedom of many Republic worlds, the Jedi have become reluctant soldiers in the fight against the Confederacy's droid armies.

obi-wan kenobi

The former Padawan of Jedi Master Qui-Gon Jinn, Obi-Wan Kenobi honored his Master's last request to train young Anakin Skywalker in the ways of the Force. Obi-Wan is a skilled fighter and has survived two previous encounters with the Jedi's most deadly nemesis, the Sith Lords.

Following the Battle of Geonosis, Obi-Wan became not only a Jedi Master but also a general in the Grand Army of the Republic. With thousands of clone troopers at his command, he led the Jedi forces against the Confederacy's attack of the cloning facilities on the planet Kamino. He was also instrumental in stopping a Confederacy chemical weapons program on Queyta, and in capturing San Hill, a key Confederacy leader, on the banking world of Muunilinst.

Playing obi-wan
Ewan McGregor

Birthday: *March 31, 1971*
Birthplace: *Crieff, Scotland, UK*
Film debut: *Being Human (1993)*
Ewan McGregor studied Alec Guinness's performance as the aged Obi-Wan in the first *Star Wars* trilogy, and also watched many of Guinness's other films to emulate his voice and mannerisms. "The step between the end of Episode III and the beginning of Episode IV has to be one that you can believe."

"You Fought in the Clone Wars?"

The first mention of the Clone Wars occurred in *A New Hope*, when Luke Skywalker (Mark Hamill) asked old Ben Kenobi (Alec Guinness) about his past. The Clone Wars commenced when an army of clones fought alongside the Jedi against the Separatists' droids on the planet Geonosis. Following the theatrical release of *Attack of the Clones*, the Clone Wars continued as a multimedia project that included animated cartoons, comics, books, toys, and games.

ANAKIN, OBI-WAN, AND MACE FROM THE CARTOON NETWORK'S ANIMATED SERIES STAR WARS: CLONE WARS

anakin skywalker

Once a slave, Anakin Skywalker was discovered on the planet Tatooine by the Jedi Master Qui-Gon Jinn. Qui-Gon quickly realized that Anakin possessed great power, and he believed the boy was destined to fulfill a prophecy and bring balance to the Force.

Anakin's powers have grown stronger over the years. At age twenty-three, he has become one of the best starfighter pilots in the galaxy. Although he has only been a Jedi Knight for six months, Supreme Chancellor Palpatine has appointed Anakin to the Jedi Council as his personal representative.

Unfortunately, Anakin does not always honor the Jedi code of conduct. Instead, he often allows his feelings to dictate his actions. Because of his sporadic displays of anger and pride, the Jedi Council deems him not ready for the title of Jedi Master. Anakin is resentful of the Jedi Council and torn by their demands. He is even more tormented by his forbidden love for Padmé Amidala, whom he secretly married after the Battle of Geonosis.

playing anakin
Hayden Christensen

Birthday: *April 19, 1981*
Birthplace: *Vancouver, British Columbia, Canada*
Film debut: *In the Mouth of Madness* (1995)
To mold himself into a combat-hardened Jedi, Hayden Christensen physically trained for over a month before starting principal photography. He maintained a daily regimen of six-hour lightsaber dueling drills followed by a two-hour workout.

But what was it like to turn evil? In a BBC interview, Christensen said, "Playing a character that has those darker elements, you do learn more about yourself and your own qualities when you're figuring out a way to motivate yourself for those scenes."

How Did Anakin Get That Nasty Scar?

"I don't know," George Lucas admitted during the film's production. *"I just put it there. I think Anakin got it slipping in the bathtub, but of course, he's not going to tell anybody that."* Subsequently, the comic Republic #71 revealed that a lightsaber fight with Asajj Ventress was the cause.

OBI-WAN'S LIGHTSABER

ANAKIN'S LIGHTSABER

Lightsabers

The traditional weapon of the Jedi, lightsabers are used to deflect incoming blaster bolts and can cut through almost anything. A control button triggers the projection of a meter-long blade of pure energy. The blade's color is determined by crystals that focus energy from the lightsaber's power cells through the lens at the center of the handle. Although they are strictly reserved for use by Jedi, lightsabers are also used by their enemy, the Sith.

comlink

When the Jedi infiltrate the Trade Federation cruiser to rescue Chancellor Palpatine, Obi-Wan uses this communication device to contact R2-D2.

electrobinoculars

Stalking an enemy on the planet Utapau, Obi-Wan uses his multisensor binoculars to scan a high-rise building.

breather

Obi-Wan utilizes this breathing device after he plunges into a water-filled sinkhole on Utapau.

"Your Father's Lightsaber."

To maintain continuity between films, prop master Ty Teiger constructed Anakin Skywalker's lightsaber to match the one that Ben Kenobi gives to Luke in *Star Wars*: Episode IV *A New Hope*. The original lightsaber prop's parts consisted of an antique Graflex 3-cell camera flash (commonly used by newspaper photographers in the 1940s), a light emitting diode (LED) display from a 1974 calculator that slid into the flash's mounting clamp, black handgrips, and a D-ring assembly so the prop could be clipped to a belt.

To make Luke's lightsaber appear as a glowing beam of energy, a spinning wooden "blade" was partly coated with reflective material, then carefully illuminated and photographed through a half-silvered mirror. Since *The Phantom Menace*, lightsabers have been constructed with metal blades and illuminated by computer-generated effects in post-production.

ANAKIN USES HIS LIGHTSABER TO CUT A HOLE IN AN ELEVATOR CEILING.

"Flying is for droids!" —Obi-Wan

Jedi starfighter

Obi-Wan's red Jedi starfighter is more maneuverable than his former single-person fighter craft, the Delta-7 *Aethersprite* light interceptor. One holdover from the Delta-7 is the astromech droid R4-P17. It has been remodeled from a hardwired head to a full-bodied droid, capable of independent movement from the ship.

mace windu and Yoda

"The Jedi Council wants this war to end."
—Mace Windu

mace windu

After spending many years stationed at the Jedi Temple as a senior member of the High Council, Mace Windu was forced back into action during the Clone Wars. Although he was not entirely at ease with the way the Jedi had become military leaders, he saw no other way to restore peace.

Mace is a master of the Form VII discipline of combat, also known as Vaapad. Because this deadly fighting technique leans toward the practices of the dark side of the Force, it is used by only the most skilled Jedi.

playing mace
Samuel L. Jackson
Birthday: December 21, 1948
Birthplace: Washington, D.C., USA
Film debut: Together for Days (1972)
A lifelong fan of swashbuckler films, Samuel L. Jackson was thrilled to be cast in *Star Wars.* "The fact that you're in something that is really high adventure, that's fanciful, that's exciting, that's fast-paced, that allows an audience member to experience something that we wouldn't normally experience, and actually be inspired to a point that you dream about this stuff—that's great!"

"Destroy the Sith, we must." —Yoda

yoda

During the Clone Wars, nearly all of the Jedi, including Yoda, became generals. However, some Jedi disagreed with the politics of the war, and they protested by abandoning the Jedi Order. This turn of events left Yoda gravely concerned, for he knew that dissension in the Jedi ranks would make the Jedi Order appear weak to the public and more vulnerable to its enemies.

Yoda led the charge against the Separatists on Muunilinst. He also went to Vjun in an attempt to peacefully resolve the war with Count Dooku, but the mission was nothing more than a tainted trick by Dooku. Yoda continues to try to ease tensions between the Senate and the Wookiees, doing everything in his power to keep the Wookiee homeworld, Kashyyyk, within the Republic and safe from the Confederacy.

Playing yoda
Frank Oz

Birthday: May 25, 1944
Birthplace: Hereford, England, UK
Film debut: The Muppet Movie (1979)
Before he became a director of feature films, Frank Oz was famed for his puppeteering work on Sesame Street and The Muppet Show. He controlled and voiced Yoda puppets for The Empire Strikes Back, Return of the Jedi, and The Phantom Menace.

the original yoda

For The Empire Strikes Back, Yoda was a foam latex puppet sculpted by makeup and special-creature designer Stuart Freeborn, who combined elements of his own features with Albert Einstein's eyes to create Yoda's head. Freeborn relied on his knowledge of engineering to figure out the mechanisms to control the puppet's eyes, mouth, and ears. "The first time George [Lucas] saw it, he said, 'That's it, that's the way I want it,' and from there on, I didn't change anything else."

However, Freeborn's other makeup duties precluded the possibility of him being Yoda's puppeteer. "I told [Empire producer] Gary Kurtz that I wasn't going to have time to sit there and operate Yoda, so I had to have somebody else. He asked me who I'd like and I told him that for my money the best man for the job was Frank Oz."

STUART FREEBORN

THE JEDI COUNCIL RELUCTANTLY ACCEPTS ANAKIN'S APPOINTMENT AS CHANCELLOR PALPATINE'S PERSONAL REPRESENTATIVE.

For many centuries, the Jedi Council was made up of twelve Jedi Masters who resided in the towering Jedi Temple on Coruscant. During the Clone Wars, most Jedi were assigned to protect distant worlds across the galaxy, and the Council became fragmented. Hologram transmissions were used to maintain contact between the scattered Jedi generals.

Jedi Generals

Two hundred Jedi fought at the Battle of Geonosis. Few survived, but those who did joined the 10,000 Jedi scattered throughout the galaxy to serve the Republic during the Clone Wars. Despite the fact that some Jedi are especially skilled fighters, they use their power cautiously, always hoping for peace.

Agen Kolar

A Zabrak Jedi, Agen Kolar believes that service to the Republic is the foundation of Jedi duty. As a general in the Clone Wars, he leads troopers to assist Shaak Ti on Brentaal IV.

Unlike most members of the Jedi Council, the telepathic Iktotchi Saesee Tiin has a great interest in technology. Using his knowledge in combination with his Jedi powers, he is able to pilot his starfighter without a nav computer and can instinctively astrogate his way through lightspeed.

MACE WINDU, AGEN KOLAR, AND SAESEE TIIN ENTER THE SENATE OFFICE BUILDING TO TAKE A SITH LORD INTO CUSTODY.

Ki-Adi-Mundi

A member of the Jedi Council, the Cerean Ki-Adi-Mundi has been assigned to the crystal world of Mygeeto.

Plo Koon

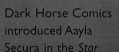

Also a Jedi Council member, the Kel Dor Plo Koon fights the Clone Wars on Cato Neimoidia.

Kit Fisto

An amphibious native of Glee Anselm, Kit Fisto wields a lightsaber that has two crystals that work on a bifurcating cyclical-ignition pulse, allowing the weapon to function underwater.

Stass Allie

Cousin to Adi Gallia, the experienced warrior Stass Allie is increasingly devoted to the Circle of Jedi Healers.

Aayla Secura

A Twi'lek from the planet Ryloth, Aayla Secura has had near-fatal encounters with both General Grievous and the notorious bounty hunter Aurra Sing. She has been assigned to protect the planet Felucia.

Dark Horse Comics introduced Aayla Secura in the *Star Wars: Twilight* miniseries, written by John Ostrander and illustrated by Jan Duursema. Aayla quickly became a fan favorite and was later illustrated by artist John Foster for the cover of the comic *Star Wars #33*. George Lucas saw the cover art and decided to add Aayla to the Geonosis battle sequence in *Attack of the Clones,* then incorporated her into *Revenge of the Sith.* In both films, Amy Allen played Secura. At one time, Amy was a production assistant for Industrial Light & Magic, George Lucas's special-effects company.

What's a Hologram?

Holography is the technique of producing images by waveform reconstruction. Lasers are used to record an image on a photographic plate to create a diffraction pattern (an organized arrangement of light) that can be projected to appear as an object with the characteristics of height, width, and depth. These light-generated three-dimensional images are called holograms.

"Now you will experience the full power of the dark side."
—Darth Sidious

Sith

Thousands of years before the Clone Wars, the Jedi clashed with the Sith Lords, who used the Force for evil. Though the Sith's numbers were decimated, they managed to survive by operating in pairs. Through the years, Masters and apprentices bided their time until they could exact their revenge on the Jedi.

According to legend, there was once a Dark Lord of the Sith named Darth Plagueis. He was so powerful that he could use the Force to create life and prevent death. His only fear was that he might lose his power. He was murdered by his own apprentice, who knew all of his Master's secrets.

darth sidious

From his shadowy lair on Coruscant, the Sith Lord Darth Sidious manipulates people and events to achieve his nefarious goals. Although he knows the Jedi are aware of his existence, he is confident that his arcane knowledge of the dark side of the Force will enable him to defeat all his enemies. His quest for power will not be complete until he controls the entire galaxy.

count dooku

Ten years before the beginning of the Clone Wars, the idealist Jedi Master Count Dooku abandoned the Jedi Order. While most Jedi believed Dooku had gone into seclusion, he had in fact been enlisted as an apprentice by Darth Sidious. Dooku was renamed Darth Tyranus.

The new Sith Lord assassinated the Jedi Master Sifo-Dyas, who had been sent by Chancellor Palpatine to Kamino to secretly commission a clone army. Dooku then presented himself as Lord Tyranus and recruited Jango Fett to be the genetic source for the clones.

After a decade of covert activity, Dooku resurfaced as the leader of the Separatist movement. On Geonosis, he told a captive Obi-Wan Kenobi that the Senate was under the control of the Sith Lord Darth Sidious. He fought with the Jedi before making a daring escape into space.

playing count dooku

Christopher Lee

Birthday: May 27, 1922
Birthplace: Belgravia, London, England, UK
In a career that has spanned more than half a century, Christopher Lee has accumulated more film credits than any other actor, including the role of Saruman the White in *The Lord of the Rings* trilogy. How does Lee compare Saruman with Dooku? "In *The Lord of the Rings,* I'm a wizard, but in a *Star Wars* film, I am a part of the wizardry and magic of the whole thing."

PETER CUSHING

Frankenstein vs. Sith Lords

Actor Peter Cushing (Grand Moff Tarkin in *Star Wars*) played the scientist Victor Frankenstein in several British horror films, including *The Curse of Frankenstein* (1957), in which Frankenstein's monster was played by Christopher Lee (Darth Tyranus), and *Frankenstein and the Monster from Hell* (1974), in which the monster was played by David Prowse (Darth Vader in the *Star Wars* trilogy).

DAVID PROWSE AND
SIR ALEC GUINNESS

ANAKIN BATTLES COUNT DOOKU ON GENERAL GRIEVOUS'S COMMAND SHIP.

...AND TODAY, I GET TO KILL *FOUR* OF YOU.

ADD TO THAT THE GUNGANS I *ALREADY* MURDERED, THE HOSTAGES I'M GOING TO KILL *LATER*, AND ALL THE NABOO WHO WILL DIE *TOMORROW*, AND IT'S A DAMN GOOD WEEK.

The Clone Wars developed and introduced two new villains to the *Star Wars* universe. Although they do not appear in *Revenge of the Sith*, their popularity demands inclusion here.

asajj ventress

On the remote, barbaric world of Rattatak, a stranded Jedi named Ky Narec discovered a young orphan. The child, named Asajj Ventress, was strong in the Force. Narec became Ventress's teacher, but he was killed by warlords. His former pupil developed a hatred for the Republic and turned to the dark side.

Years later, when Count Dooku sought out planets to join the Separatists, he ventured to Rattatak and found Ventress. Recognizing her talents, Dooku enlisted her to join his fight against the Jedi. He gave her twin curved-handled lightsabers that can be joined to form a double-bladed weapon. Though she aspired to be a Sith, Ventress came to be known only as a Dark Jedi. She did achieve the rank of commander in the Separatist army.

PLANET RATTATAK

Durge

A two-thousand-year-old Gen'Dai bounty hunter with a scattered nervous system, Durge is completely encased in battered high-impact armor. Over the ages, he learned the fighting techniques of his many enemies, including the Jedi Knights. He was recruited by Count Dooku, who knew that Durge would enjoy indulging his bloodlust on the Jedi as well as the Republic clones.

Following Dooku's directives, Durge created an elite rapid-deployment military force to protect Confederacy planets. He led his droid forces against the Republic army on the planet Muunilinst, but was ultimately bested by Obi-Wan Kenobi.

general grievous

Born a Kaleesh, Grievous had already achieved notoriety and his general's rank when he was fatally wounded in a shuttle crash. His story might have ended there, had not the InterGalactic Banking Clan been seeking a master strategist to lead its droids against the Republic. Rather than spend his final days suspended in the healing fluids of a bacta tank, he accepted the Clan's offer to utilize Geonosian cyborg technology that would allow him not only to walk again but also be stronger and faster than ever.

Grievous's physical remains were installed within an incredibly hard type of ceramic armor shell, and his mechanical enhancements gave him an edge in fighting in close quarters. He was soon introduced to Count Dooku, who trained him in lightsaber technique. Now the supreme commander of the droid armies, he is distinguished by having killed more Jedi in hand-to-hand combat than any other being.

GRIEVOUS'S
WHEEL BIKE

"I look forward to adding your lightsaber to my collection."
—General Grievous

An Uneasy Alliance

What would General Grievous do if he discovered it was not mere circumstance that caused his shuttle crash and rebirth as a mechanized life-form? In fact, Count Dooku orchestrated General Grievous's transformation into the perfect leader for the droid armies. Although Grievous has proven to be a capable Jedi killer, Count Dooku deplores the cyborg's ungallant habit of collecting lightsabers. Dooku also disapproves of Grievous's penchant for using multiple lightsabers in combat, as a skilled duelist should be able to manage with only one.

Droid Magnaguards

Although Grievous is more than capable of defending himself, he seldom travels without his droid bodyguards, who are prepared to destroy anything that poses a threat to their master.

Drawing Board

After George Lucas instructed the Episode III art department to create an alien or droid general, concept artists Alex Jaeger, T.J. Frame, Erik Tiemens, Iain McCaig, Derek Thompson, Feng Zhu, Sang Jun Lee, and Warren Fu went to work creating ideas for the cyborg who would come to be known as General Grievous. Finding inspiration for Grievous's face from the form of the top of a plastic spray bottle, Fu made sketches. Ryan Church and Iain McCaig refined Fu's sketches, and Robert Barnes made a foot-tall clay maquette, a sculpture to help the designers and the director see the character from all sides.

Once Lucas approved Grievous's design, the maquette was scanned into a computer to become the basis of a wire-frame model that would be used for animation. According to animation director Rob Coleman, Grievous was "so complicated that the modeler had to go and build everything by hand inside the computer. It's the most complicated creature we've ever built." Grievous ultimately appears in the film as a fully rendered, computer-generated character.

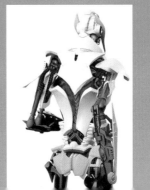

droid tri-fighter

Approximately 5.5 meters long, a tri-fighter has no crew or passengers and runs on an integrated droid brain.

droid gunship

This ground-assault fighter is designed to demolish ground-based installations and attack vehicles with its laser cannons and concussion bombs.

trade federation cruiser

The Trade Federation cruiser *Invisible Hand* is under General Grievous's command when Chancellor Palpatine is kidnapped and held prisoner there.

vulture droids

Variable-geometry robotic spacecraft, these starfighters are able to turn, fold, and transform into different configurations.

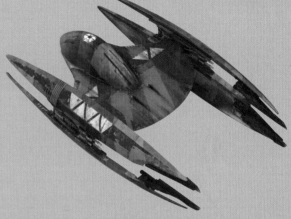

super droid R77

One of many super droids, R77 serves on board the Trade Federation cruiser that functions as General Grievous's command ship.

Deployed in the form of silver balls, buzz droids open to reveal spider-like legs. The legs attach themselves to enemy vehicles, then sharp-edged appendages shred through hull plating and wiring.

republic clone trooper army

The Republic's clone army was genetically engineered in special facilities on Kamino. The Kaminoans used incredible growth-acceleration technology to raise this army in just fifteen years. The clones are identical, entirely fearless, and trained to obey their commanding officers without question. The regular army consists of over one million clone troopers. Color-coded flashes on the armor indicate rank.

chain of command

The army's supreme commander is Supreme Chancellor Palpatine. He meets regularly with the Jedi, who have been appointed Republic generals. Each Jedi general has been assigned a clone commander, who supervises both the regular army of clone troopers and the commando units.

DC-15 rifle

The standard-issue blaster rifle for clone troopers, the DC-15 fires charged plasma bolts. Although this type of weapon frees soldiers from the need to carry projectile ammunition, blasters are notoriously hard to aim due to plasma bolts' inherently unstable nature.

ARC troopers

Before his untimely demise, Jango Fett hand-trained a group of clone troopers that were designated Advance Recon Commandos. When the Separatists attacked Kamino, Prime Minister Lama Su personally activated the ARC troopers to defend Tipoca City. Genetically engineered to be capable of a substantial amount of independent thought, an ARC trooper armed with a portable missile launcher could take out enemy vehicles and fortifications by himself. Because only a finite number of ARC troopers were trained by Jango Fett, they were used sparingly during the Clone Wars.

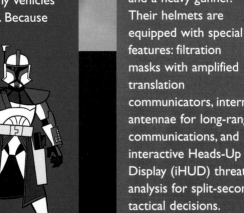

Republic commandos

The commando units are made up of clones who have been genetically modified to handle the stress and aggression of unorthodox combat tactics. Each unit includes a sniper, a demolitions specialist, and a heavy gunner. Their helmets are equipped with special features: filtration masks with amplified translation communicators, internal antennae for long-range communications, and interactive Heads-Up Display (iHUD) threat analysis for split-second tactical decisions.

Instead of the DC-15, Republic commandos use the DC-17m rifle, which has a modifiable chassis that quickly transforms the weapon into a sniper rifle or anti-armor gun.

Working directly with the Jedi generals on worlds throughout the galaxy, the clone commanders have proven themselves to be infinitely reliable and loyal soldiers. Although some Jedi initially felt awkward in leading the troops, most ultimately took comfort in knowing their backs were covered by the fearless commanders.

clone swamp speeder

Used to travel over wet terrain, such as the lagoons of Kashyyyk.

ARC-170 starfighter

This heavily armed Aggressive ReConnaissance fighter can reach speeds up to 9,600 kph (5,965 mph).

Clone Commander Cody (2224) serves
Obi-Wan on Utapau.

Clone Commander Bacara (1138) serves
Ki-Adi-Mundi on the crystal world of Mygeeto.

Clone Commander Gree (1004) serves
Yoda on Kashyyyk.

Clone Commander Bly (5052) serves
Aayla Secura on Felucia.

Clone Commander Appo (1119) and Clone Trooper Fox (1010)
are stationed at the Jedi Temple on Coruscant.

Mandalorian Inspiration

Just as Jango Fett was the clone army's genetic host, his Mandalorian armor gave inspiration to the heavy-duty shell-like coverings that were worn by the clones at the Battle of Geonosis. The clone trooper helmets' "T" visor plates were adapted with enhanced breath filters for battle conditions.

Playing commander cody
Temuera Morrison

Birthday: December 1961
Birthplace: Rotorua, New Zealand
Film debut: *Rangi's Catch* (1972)
In *Attack of the Clones,* Temuera Morrison played Jango Fett, the bounty hunter who was the genetic source for the clone army. In *Revenge of the Sith,* he plays Clone Commander Cody. Although Morrison appears to be wearing the armor of a clone commander, the actor's head was digitally combined with a computer-generated armored body.

clone BARC speeder

Clone scouts use BARC speeder bikes on planets such as Felucia and Coruscant.

Look Familiar?

No, it's not an Imperial snowtrooper on vacation but a pre-production Boba Fett costume for *The Empire Strikes Back,* which was designed by art director for visual effects Joe Johnston and conceptual artist Ralph McQuarrie. According to Johnston, "Originally, Boba Fett was part of a force we called super troopers, and they were these really high-tech fighting units, and they all looked alike. That eventually evolved into a single bounty hunter."

v-wing starfighter

This clone fighter has an astromech droid and dual laser cannons.

the senate

> "There are times when we must all endure adjustment to the Constitution in the name of security."
> —Chancellor Palpatine

In shambles after decades of corruption, the Senate is increasingly divided over the fate of the Galactic Republic. While some Senators argue over whether the war against the Separatists is justified, most are merely concerned with protecting their own interests.

supreme chancellor palpatine

It seems strange that a man who claims to be mild by nature has become the most powerful individual in the Galactic Senate, but Palpatine would be the first to point out that it wasn't entirely his doing. The former Senator of Naboo can thank Padmé Amidala for casting a vote of "no confidence" for his predecessor, Chancellor Valorum. He can also thank Jar Jar Binks for proposing that the Senate should give him emergency powers to create an army for the Republic to fight the Separatists.

Following the Battle of Geonosis, Palpatine maintained that he would relinquish his emergency powers when the Separatist threat was over. But as the Clone Wars progressed, even Palpatine's most trusted friends and supporters were surprised by his many amendments to the Republic Constitution. He was extending his own political powers while limiting the freedom of others. Although these actions have prompted the Jedi Council to become suspicious of the Supreme Chancellor's goals, Anakin believes Palpatine truly cares about the fate of the Republic.

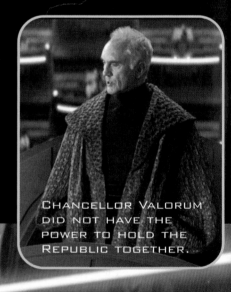

CHANCELLOR VALORUM DID NOT HAVE THE POWER TO HOLD THE REPUBLIC TOGETHER.

WAR TEARS THROUGH THE GALAXY AS THE SENATE DECIDES ITS FATE.

Playing Palpatine

Ian McDiarmid

Birthday: August 11, 1944
Birthplace: Carnoustie, Tayside, Scotland, UK
Film debut: The Likely Lads (1976)

Having played Emperor Palpatine in *Return of the Jedi*, Ian McDiarmid is well aware of his character's ultimate goals. "He's the great political manipulator of all time. I imagine he's evil from birth, which is a terrible thing to imagine. He's not human." McDiarmid has also acted under the direction of Frank Oz (Yoda) in *Dirty Rotten Scoundrels* (1988) and appeared with Christopher Lee (Count Dooku) and Ray Park (Darth Maul) in *Sleepy Hollow*.

sly moore

Aide to Supreme Chancellor Palpatine, Sly Moore is an Umbaran. Like all her people, she is reputed to have the ability to influence the minds of others. She is rumored to know Palpatine's darkest secrets.

mas Amedda

Mas Amedda is Vice Chair of the Galactic Senate. A Chagrian, his blue skin screens out the harmful radiation from the sun of his homeworld, Champala.

senator padmé amidala

Born Padmé Naberrie, Padmé took the last name Amidala when she was Queen of Naboo. She became Senator of Naboo after Palpatine left that position to become Chancellor. During the rise of the Separatist movement, Padmé's efforts to urge diplomatic solutions over military buildup made her unpopular with those who supported the Military Creation Act.

Four months into the Clone Wars, Padmé helped Yoda travel to the frigid world of Ilum after he sensed a disturbance in the Force. She would like to do more to help the Jedi, but Nute Gunray has placed a colossal bounty on her head. Padmé is forced to mostly stay on Coruscant or Naboo. Fortunately, she has found a small group of good friends among the Senators, including Bail Organa and Mon Mothma.

Like Anakin, Padmé has long wished that their marriage did not have to be a secret. When she learns that she is pregnant, she realizes that the secret will soon be impossible to keep.

playing padmé
Natalie Portman

Birthday: June 9, 1981
Birthplace: Jerusalem, Israel
Film debut: *Léon*, also released as *The Professional* (1994)

With *The Phantom Menace* and *Attack of the Clones* behind her, Natalie Portman was experienced with working on blue-screen sets, where various invisible elements—everything from the surrounding buildings, vehicles, and other characters—were computer-generated in post-production. Portman describes "blue-screen acting" as "maybe the purest form of acting, because it's like being a little kid in a cardboard box and thinking it's a spaceship. That's the point you have to get to—pure imagination."

captain typho

Captain Typho is the head of security for Senator Amidala. He was a Junior Palace Guard when he lost his left eye bravely fighting Trade Federation droids during the Battle of Naboo.

LEFT TO RIGHT: HAYDEN CHRISTENSEN, RICK MCCALLUM, GEORGE LUCAS, NATALIE PORTMAN, AND EWAN MCGREGOR

OBI-WAN COMFORTS PADMÉ AS HER HUSBAND TURNS TO THE DARK SIDE.

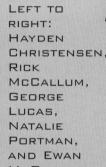

ANAKIN'S DESIRE TO KEEP PADMÉ SAFE PUSHES HIM INTO THE ARMS OF THE EMPEROR.

The Delegation of Two Thousand

"We can't let a thousand years of democracy disappear without a fight."
—Bail Organa

Alarmed by Chancellor Palpatine's numerous amendments to the Republic Constitution, a group of Senators meet clandestinely to discuss their concerns. This alliance— eventually calling itself the Delegation of Two Thousand— seeks a diplomatic solution to the war and an end to Chancellor Palpatine's Constitutional amendments.

Bail Organa

Senator Bail Organa is—along with Mon Mothma— one of the founding members of the Delegation of Two Thousand. He is also the head of the royal family of Alderaan and bears the title of Viceroy and First Chairman. Although Organa has no direct heirs, he and his wife have often talked about adopting a baby.

Playing Bail
Jimmy Smits

Birthday: July 9, 1955
Birthplace: Brooklyn, New York, USA
Film debut: Running Scared (1986)
Well known for his award-winning performances on *LA Law* and *NYPD Blue*, Jimmy Smits returns as Bail Organa.

Now and Then: Mon Mothma

In *Revenge of the Sith,* Mon Mothma is played by
Genevieve O'Reilly, who appeared as Officer Wirtz
in *The Matrix Reloaded* and *The Matrix Revolutions.* In
Return of the Jedi, Mon Mothma, the leader of the
Rebel Alliance, was played by Caroline Blakiston.

mon mothma

The daughter of an arbiter-general and a planetary
governor, Senator Mon Mothma represents
Chandrila, an agricultural world in the Bormea sector.

"We are not Separatists, trying to leave the Republic.
We are loyalists, trying to preserve democracy in the
Republic." —Mon Mothma

malé Dee

Malé Dee's unique appearance
is enhanced by Visdic body
wrappings. His hairstyle is a
plea for peace.

nee Alavar

Nee Alavar is played by Rena
Owen, the voice of Taun We in
Attack of the Clones.

fang zar

Fang Zar's beard and
Sern Prime topknot are
symbols of status among
his people.

C-3PO and R2-D2

C-3PO

Built by young Anakin Skywalker from scavenged parts, the protocol droid C-3PO resembled little more than an ambulatory skeleton when Anakin left Tatooine. C-3PO continued to live with Anakin's mother, Shmi, after she married Cliegg Lars. Much to the self-conscious droid's relief, Shmi covered his "naked" form of exposed circuits and wires with metal plating.

Ten years passed before C-3PO met his "maker" again, when Anakin returned to Tatooine in a desperate attempt to rescue Shmi from Tusken Raiders. Anakin failed in his effort, but he took C-3PO with him when he left the planet.

After witnessing the secret wedding of Anakin and Padmé, the droid became a trusted servant to both. On Coruscant, he is in charge of Padmé's apartment.

playing C-3PO
Anthony Daniels

Birthday: *February 21, 1946*
Birthplace: *Salisbury, England, UK*
Film debut: *Star Wars* (1977)

George Lucas originally imagined C-3PO speaking with a Brooklyn accent and having the attitude of a used-car dealer, but he was ultimately won over by actor Anthony Daniels's interpretation of the character as a nervous English butler. According to Daniels, "Threepio, being pure machine, is utterly confused by things like the Force and people kissing—anything that is non-mechanical, Threepio doesn't get it. He's aware, sadly, of something that he doesn't have but humans do—probably a heart, though he doesn't understand affection. His own brand of loyalty comes pretty close. He's a very confused person."

Anthony Daniels has worn the C-3PO costume in all the *Star Wars* films. Like R2-D2, C-3PO is also sometimes a computer-generated image. Besides playing C-3PO in the *Star Wars* films, Daniels has also leant his voice to the golden droid in the *Star Wars* radio dramas for National Public Radio, Star Tours for Walt Disney World, numerous audiobooks and games, and the animated series *Droids* and *Clone Wars*.

R2-D2

Formerly an emergency astromech droid on Queen Amidala's Royal Starship, R2-D2 has proven that he is more imaginative, resourceful, and loyal than the average starship-repair droid. His body houses numerous tools and devices, and concealed booster rockets allow limited flight. Although he still belongs to Padmé, he has been transferred to Anakin in the past six months of the Clone Wars.

Inside R2-D2

Kenny Baker no longer has to climb inside the R2-D2 costume, except for old times' sake. A remote-controlled R2 is used for shots where he's interacting with actors on the set. A digital R2 is used for stunts.

The remote-controlled R2-D2 is maintained and operated by the Droid Unit. Led by Don Bies, the team includes droid technicians Justin Dix, Matt Sloan (who also plays the Jedi Master Plo Koon), and unit coordinator Zeynep "Zed" Selcuk. When R2-D2 is required to haul a heavy load, the team uses a model nicknamed AT-R2 (All-Terrain Artoo), which is equipped with powerful wheelchair motors.

THE DROID WRANGLING TEAM

From space, the windswept planet Utapau appears to have a dimpled surface. Upon closer inspection, the "dimples" are massive sinkholes that are linked by tunnels. Rather than attempt to level the wildly uneven land areas, the Utapauns have constructed their cities in and around the towering cliffs that line the sinkholes. They harness energy via large windmills.

Because Utapau had few natural resources that were desired by the Confederacy of Independent Systems, the planet managed to remain within the fold of the Republic during most of the Clone Wars. But when the Separatist leaders took refuge on Utapau, they inevitably brought the war with them.

utapau mount

In need of transportation, Obi-Wan commandeers a giant lizard named Boga from a corral. With her powerful legs, Boga is able to cross rough terrain and climb sheer cliffs.

nute gunray
Viceroy of the Trade Federation, he doubts General Grievous's ability to keep the Separatists safe.

rune haako
Lieutenant of the Trade Federation

poggle the lesser
Archduke of Geonosis

shu mai
Presidente of the Commerce Guild

OBI-WAN CONFRONTS GRIEVOUS ON THE TENTH LEVEL OF THE UTAPAU CITY.

"Surely you realize you're doomed." —General Grievous

THE NOS MONSTER LIVES IN UTAPAU'S UNDERWATER CAVES.

tion medon

A local administrator, the Utapaun Tion Medon greets Obi-Wan on a landing platform.

Which Came First: Tatooine or Utapau?

Utapau is not entirely new to the *Star Wars* universe. Its name dates back to 1973, when George Lucas used it in his rough and first drafts of *Star Wars*. In those drafts, the fourth moon of Utapau was inhabited by the story's original hero, a sixteen-year-old boy named Annikin Starkiller. In subsequent drafts, Utapau was a desert planet with two suns, and the hero's name was changed to Luke Starkiller. By the final draft, the desert planet was Tatooine, and the hero was Luke Skywalker.

san hill

Chairman of the InterGalactic Banking Clan

po nudo

The planet Ando's Separatist Senator

wat tambor

Foreman of the Techno Union

passel argente

Senator of Kooriva and Magistrate of the Corporate Alliance

A jungle planet covered with kilometers-high wroshyr trees and murky lagoons, Kashyyyk is the homeworld of the tall, fur-covered Wookiees. Although the Wookiees have incorporated modern technology into their society, they often opt to use traditional tools to maintain their cities and protect their environment.

The Separatists want to add Kashyyyk to the Confederacy of Independent Systems. As Yoda is an old friend to the Wookiees, he leads the clone troops to protect Kashyyyk from the droid armies.

wookiee escape pod

Equipped with an engine that can achieve escape velocity, this emergency escape pod is used by Yoda for a discreet departure from Kashyyyk.

wookiee flying catamaran

This marvel of engineering allows Wookiee warriors to bombard Separatist ground forces from the relative safety of the craft's dual hulls.

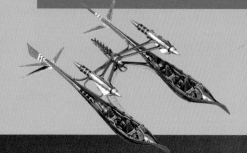

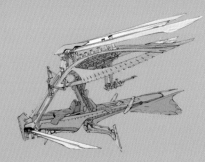

wookiee "Gnasp" flyer

A single-seat flying craft used by the Wookiees to defend against the Separatist invasion of Kashyyyk, this is known as a Raddadugh "Gnasp" fluttercraft.

TARFFUL LEADS A FIERCE WOOKIEE ARMY TO REPEL SEPARATIST INVADERS.

chewbacca

A 2.28-meter-tall Wookiee, Chewbacca fought alongside Yoda to defend his homeworld against the droid armies. Though the Clone Wars have made the future uncertain for many, Chewbacca is destined to become the copilot of the *Millennium Falcon* and a hero of the future Rebel Alliance.

Tarfful

A ferocious fighter, Tarfful is the leader of Chewbacca's clan. He has been friends with Yoda since long before the Clone Wars.

playing chewbacca

Peter Mayhew

Birthday: *May 19, 1944*
Birthplace: *Barnes, England, UK*
Film debut: *Star Wars* (1977)

"I'm delighted to return as Chewbacca," said actor Peter Mayhew, who played the famous Wookiee in the *Star Wars* trilogy. "I think his reappearance in this film is a fitting way to tie the whole saga together, especially for Wookiee fans." Asked about Chewbacca's enduring popularity, Mayhew said, "He's not articulate in speech, but he expresses what everybody else is feeling. And the mere fact that he's cuddly and nice appeals to all ages, from kids upwards. He's a teddy bear. He's totally soft and lovable, but he can also be nasty. I think it just appeals to people's nature."

R. M'QUARRIE

Where Did the Word "Wookiee" Come From?

Terry McGovern was working as a voice-over actor on George Lucas's first feature film, *THX-1138*. As the character THX stole a car, McGovern quipped, "I think I ran over a Wookiee back there!" George loved the word and later used it in *A New Hope*.

Speaking Wookiee

The man behind Chewbacca's growls and barks is sound designer Ben Burtt. "Chewbacca's voice is predominantly one bear in combination with a few other sounds, which helps to keep his voice consistent from one reel to the next."

Look Familiar?

No, it's not an Ewok tree house! This production painting by Ralph McQuarrie (opposite page) was used for the first glimpse of Chewbacca's homeworld in *The Star Wars Holiday Special*, which was televised by CBS on November 17, 1978. The show featured most of the principal actors from *Star Wars: A New Hope*, costumed actors as Chewbacca's family, and an animated cartoon that introduced Boba Fett. However, the production failed George Lucas's expectations and was never aired again.

PLANET ENDOR

The Wookiee homeworld actually dates back to Lucas's rough draft of *Star Wars* from 1973; originally, the Wookiees lived on the planet Yavin, but Yavin ultimately became the Rebels' secret base in *Star Wars: A New Hope*. According to Lucas, "The Wookiee planet that I created for *Star Wars* was eventually turned into the Ewok planet [Endor] in *Return of the Jedi*. I basically cut the Wookiees in half and called them Ewoks!

"I didn't make Endor a Wookiee planet because Chewbacca was sophisticated technologically and I wanted the characters involved in the battle to be primitive. That's why I used Ewoks instead."

EWOKS

wookiee wranglers

In Sydney, Australia, production coordinator Virginia Murray and the Episode III production team made sure everything ran smoothly for the over 700 members of the crew and cast. Murray recalled, "The biggest challenge, actually, in the beginning was the Wookiees because we had to find seven guys who are at least seven foot tall. And amazingly our extras casting director, Christine King, managed to find a few basketball players and other guys, including a prison officer. They're a real mixed bag, the Wookiees."

wookiee makeup

To create Chewbacca's mask and costume for *Star Wars* (1977), makeup designer Stuart Freeborn used real knotted hair and utilized techniques he'd pioneered for the man-apes in the film *2001: A Space Odyssey*. The original mask had a foam-rubber interior with built-in mechanisms to allow actor Peter Mayhew to open and close Chewbacca's jaws. Because age caused the foam to harden, a new mask had to be made for *Revenge of the Sith*. For the new mask, fabrication supervisor Lou Elsey used synthetic hair and the same mouth-opening mechanisms, and has incorporated small animatronics that allow Chewie to snarl, smirk, and purse his lips.

polis massa

After a brutal encounter with a Sith Lord, Yoda retreats with Bail Organa to the isolated asteroid Polis Massa. Equipped with a medical facility, Polis Massa also becomes the destination for Obi-Wan, Padmé, and the droids R2-D2 and C-3PO.

medical droid

Inside the operating room of the Polis Massa medical center, a droid assists with the emergency delivery of Padmé's twins.

POLIS MASSA MEDIC

alderaan starcruiser

A Corellian corvette, the *Tantive IV* is a consular ship registered to the Royal House of Alderaan. The 150-meter-long vessel served as Bail Organa's personal starship. It will eventually be passed on to his adopted daughter, Princess Leia, and then attacked by Darth Vader.

"We must take them someplace where the Sith will not sense their presence." —Obi-Wan

Now and Then: Captain Antilles

In *Revenge of the Sith,* Captain Antilles is played by Rohan Nichol, who was cast for his nodding resemblance with the uncredited actor who played Antilles in *A New Hope*. From the daily progress report for the first *Star Wars* film, it is believed that actor Peter Geddis played the Rebel captain who was strangled by Darth Vader on the *Tantive IV.*

THE BABIES LUKE AND LEIA

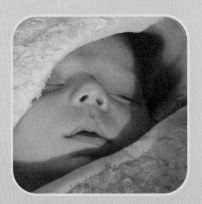

naboo star skiff

In this spacecraft, Padmé and C-3PO travel to Mustafar to find Anakin. Padmé is unaware that the skiff also carries a concealed passenger: Obi-Wan Kenobi.

The hazy, bloodred planet Mustafar is covered by active volcanoes. Despite the hostile surface conditions, a fragile settlement has been punched into the side of an obsidian mountain, transforming the area into an enormous energy-mining facility. It is here that the Separatist leaders—following the instructions of Darth Sidious—seek refuge from the Republic army.

PADMÉ AND C-3PO PREPARE TO LAND ON MUSTAFAR.

"The plan has gone as you had promised, my Lord."
—Nute Gunray

"I'll never stop loving you, but you're going down a path I cannot follow." —Padmé

"Don't you see, we don't have to run away anymore. I have brought peace to the Republic." —Anakin

the epic Battle

On Mustafar, Obi-Wan has no choice but to fight Anakin. Their friendship a thing of the past, they engage in a deadly lightsaber duel.

OBI-WAN AND ANAKIN BATTLE IN MUSTAFAR'S MAIN CONTROL CENTER.

"I see through the lies of the Jedi." —Anakin

THE DUEL CONTINUES HIGH
ABOVE A RIVER OF LAVA.

"You've let the Dark Lord twist your point of
view, until now . . . until now—you're the
very thing you swore to destroy." —Obi-Wan

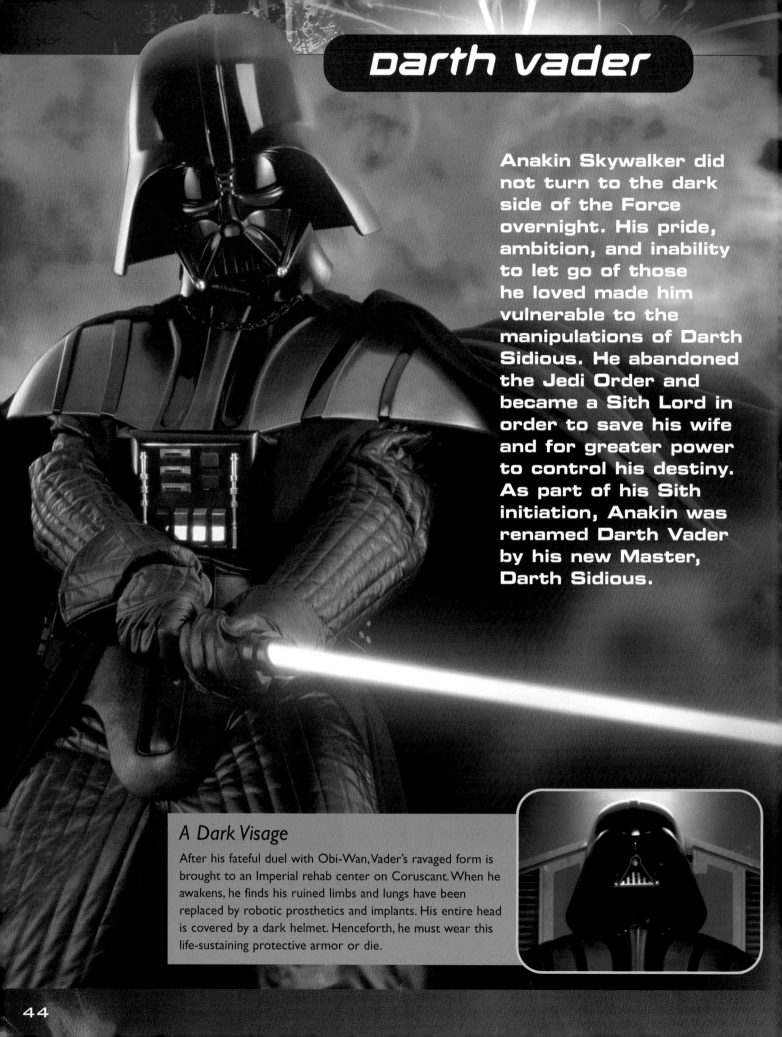

darth vader

Anakin Skywalker did not turn to the dark side of the Force overnight. His pride, ambition, and inability to let go of those he loved made him vulnerable to the manipulations of Darth Sidious. He abandoned the Jedi Order and became a Sith Lord in order to save his wife and for greater power to control his destiny. As part of his Sith initiation, Anakin was renamed Darth Vader by his new Master, Darth Sidious.

A Dark Visage

After his fateful duel with Obi-Wan, Vader's ravaged form is brought to an Imperial rehab center on Coruscant. When he awakens, he finds his ruined limbs and lungs have been replaced by robotic prosthetics and implants. His entire head is covered by a dark helmet. Henceforth, he must wear this life-sustaining protective armor or die.

Drawing Board

In 1975, George Lucas wanted several paintings to complement the *Star Wars* screenplay he intended to present to the film studio 20th Century Fox. To visualize his screenplay, he commissioned artist Ralph McQuarrie, a former technical illustrator who had previously worked with CBS News and NASA. McQuarrie wound up designing many *Star Wars* characters, including R2-D2, C-3PO, and Darth Vader.

"George said Darth Vader might have a black silk thing across his face and a big helmet like a Japanese warrior," McQuarrie recalled in an interview for *Star Wars Insider*. "The only question we had was the idea of Darth Vader not having a space suit like his stormtroopers at the point in *Star Wars* when he first appears. He is supposed to have jumped from one spaceship to another, blasted through a hole in the wall, and entered the other spaceship. I figured he couldn't have survived being in zero atmosphere, so George said give him some kind of breathing apparatus. The sort of padded, armored suit that he has on is what I conceived of as being an armored suit and a space suit with all of the life-support systems and communications systems in it."

"Until the time is right, disappear, we will." —Yoda

Hoping to prevent Darth Vader from ever discovering the existence of his offspring or locating the surviving Jedi, Yoda decides that the twins should be raised separately on distant worlds, and that he and Obi-Wan must also part ways. Obi-Wan takes Luke to Tatooine, leaving Leia under the protection of Bail Organa.

Dagobah

An obscure, sodden bog planet in the Sluis sector, Dagobah is covered by steaming bayous and petrified gnarltree forests. Its inhospitable surface is teeming with lethal life-forms and devoid of civilization, so Yoda has good reason to believe he will have few visitors to betray his location. The diminutive Jedi Master will spend the rest of his life on Dagobah.

Dagobah Origins

Before he began writing *Star Wars*, George Lucas studied stories and myths from many cultures and religions, and some of his research is evidenced by his use of modified words. The Hindi word *dagoba* means a shrine, dome-shaped structure, or mound that contains Buddhist relics. In *Star Wars*, Yoda winds up living in a dome-shaped hovel on the planet Dagobah.

Tatooine

Baked by two blazing suns, the sand planet Tatooine is—for most humans—low on the list of desirable destinations. Though it was once the home of Anakin Skywalker, it is highly doubtful that he would want to revisit the world because of the painful memories it holds for him.

Lars family homestead

Riding an eopie mount, Obi-Wan arrives at Owen and Beru Lars's moisture farm. Because Owen is Anakin's stepbrother, Obi-Wan hopes that he will agree to raise Luke as a member of his own family.

Now and Then: Owen Lars

In *Revenge of the Sith*, Owen Lars is played by Joel Edgerton. In *A New Hope*, "Uncle" Owen was played by Phil Brown.

The Clone Wars may have ended, but there are many brave souls who lament the demise of the Republic and oppose the new Empire. In time, Princess Leia Organa will become leader of the Rebel Alliance, Luke Skywalker will inherit his father's lightsaber, and the surviving Jedi will aid them in their fight against the Emperor.

The *Star Wars* are not over yet!

About the Author

Ryder Windham edited *Star Wars* titles for Dark Horse Comics before he turned to writing. Besides numerous comic strips, he has written over fifty *Star Wars* books, including *The Phantom Menace Scrapbook* and *Attack of the Clones Scrapbook* (Random House) and junior novelizations of the *Star Wars* trilogy (Scholastic). His daughters, Dorothy and Violet, have lightsabers and know how to use them.

Special thanks to the following people for their work on this book.

At Lucasfilm Ltd.:
Jonathan W. Rinzler, Senior Editor • Leland Chee, Keeper of the Holocron
Iain Morris, Art Editor • Amy Gary, Director of Publishing

At Random House Children's Books:
Lisa Findlay, Associate Editor • Cyn Constantine, Senior Designer
Godwin Chu, Copy Editor • Alison Gervais, Production Manager